Untie the "Not" in Cannot

RELEASING THE BELIEFS OF VICTIMHOOD

T.K. BANNER

PUBLISHED BY BUDDHAGOLD PRESS • MEDFORD, OREGON

Untie the "Not" in Cannot:
Releasing the Beliefs of Victimhood

by T.K. Banner

Published by BuddhaGold Press

Book Design: Chris Molé, booksavvystudio.com

ISBN: 978-0-578-79847-9

First Edition

Printed in the United States of America

This book is dedicated to
My mother
Rose Banner
1923-2020

What does it mean to be a rose?

I have to answer this, because I know my mother will not. Her name is Rose and it took many years for her roots to take hold and for her to blossom.

For many years, Rose was an enigma. She lived her entire life for others. She sacrificed for her husband, her family of orientation, and her children. Her identity was fused into those she took care of. Then the unthinkable happened; she was alone during a time of life when others should have been taking care of her.

She did discover that she was a survivor. Not content with merely existing, she forged a new life for herself even though she was terrified and believed she was incapable of being productive, especially at the age of 68. But she discarded what was now obsolete in her new life, and embraced those qualities which guaranteed her success. She even discarded her last name—only wanting to be known as "Rose."

Up until her death at the age of 96, she was still transforming herself, learning to undo the "brainwashing" as she called it (restrictions on her life, societal expectations of how a woman should behave).

Contents

FOREWORD

by B.D. Swan

Rare is the individual who does not hear the voice of "cannot" from within. This the periodical reminder from our negative side that strives to convince us that we are "less than."

T.K. Banner brilliantly shares with the reader how this negative conditioning was created by our own early programming.

More importantly we learn through these pages that is possible to quell the "cannot" voice and rise up to achieve our dreams.

Through the journey in these pages it is revealed that greatness lies within each of us. We must acknowledge the treasures we possess at the core of our being and allow our goodness to come forth.

Yes, we must chip away at the accumulation of "cannot" until our true and sparkling essence shines through.

The author proves to us we can triumph—we can truly "untie the NOT!"

INTRODUCTION

Untie the "Not" in Cannot is the result of many years of self-discovery. Because of my insecurities, and my self-absorption in my pain, I did not share my feelings with others; hence, I believed that I was different from others. I was the only one who believed I was unable to function in the real world and find passion. I spent most of my adult life, searching for answers, reading all the self-help books and seeking advice of others. I never trusted my own inner wisdom.

It was only when I really started listening to other women, and hearing their stories, did I realize we were all struggling with our identities. This insight provided me with the impetus to do more research on how we are socialized, how we are led to believe that we are "less than." I realized that for the first seven years of our lives we are programmed with information from our caregivers. This information becomes our belief system that propels us into adulthood.

We take in all new information from our environment without questioning it: we were never taught or trained in techniques of self-healing. We were never taught to dispute what we were programmed to believe. We expect our past to be our future.

Unfortunately many of us become victims of our past; we allow ourselves to be invalidated by ourselves and others.

So, over the years, I kept reading all the self-help books, attended seminars and took classes, but there was still that gaping void in my life. It wasn't until I lost everything in the fire that ravaged Paradise, California in November of 2018, that I began my journey of healing.

The fire was my blessing; I lost everything that defined me: my degrees, titles, awards and clothing. I learned the true art of "letting go." I emerged from the fire the Phoenix, completely transformed. I realized that while I read many of the self-help books, I was not applying them. "Knowledge is useless unless it is applied." Wayne Dyer made the statement that if we are identified by what own, then who are we when we don't own? What I did own was my knowledge, my personal insights from my books and education.

"Letting go" truly became my motto, my mantra. True, I was forced to let go of everything that defined me, but I was able to see the blessing in the loss. In the past two years since the fire, I have interviewed many people who lost everything in the fire. Some were absolutely stuck: they could not move forward without reliving the tragic experience. They remain victims to this day, reliving the day of the fire over and over. The experience of the fire now defines who they are. I was actually amazed that I emerged stronger and wiser. I felt like I was meeting the world naked; I had nothing to lose. I began my journey into my inner self, examining how various "voices" of parents, teachers, well-meaning friends—stunted my emotional growth. I listened to them, believed them, and acted accordingly, believing that I was "less than."

Once I truly understood how I was socialized and programmed to believe that I could not accomplish what I was destined to accomplish, I began to change. I did not need to accept that programming. I no longer needed to be a victim.

I put this belief into practice when fires raged much of Oregon in September. I watched in horror, as two towns in my vicinity were burnt to the ground: Entire trailer parks, locally owned businesses and homes all destroyed. For some of the residents, this was the second time their home was ruined by fire. As I was preparing to evacuate, it dawned on me that all I needed was my important documentation and rare photos; the rest of my belongings were just objects: There was nothing in the house I was attached to. I could let go of them.

I spent much time pondering over my first two books about the Paradise fire; again thinking about who I was before the fire and who I was after the experience. Because I emerged stronger and much more self-reflective, I decided to put my skills to use to help others who were suffering during the COVID and other crises. In the midst of a crisis, we are thrown into a state of survival, trying to meet our physical needs. Many of us do not address our emotional needs: The anger, despair, and grief that result from the devastating loss. We have to address these feelings, put them out into the open, discuss them, feel them and then finally let go. However, we are not trained to deal with our emotions; we either repress them or allow them to run amok.

Once the healing truly begins, we can embrace the feeling of non-attachment; we are not identified by our possessions. We can now really let go. In the book (and movie) *Eat, Pray, Love* it was noted that out of ruins comes transformation.

During this "new reality" isolation has become the norm for many. Mental health issues are on the rise, as is the suicide rate. It is crucial that we get the necessary assistance to cope with our loneliness. It is during this time that we can develop on new perspective: This is a time wherein we can self-reflect; we are given the opportunity to deal with personal issues and network with others who are dealing with the same issues.

We are truly not alone in feeling the pain of being cut off from the world. It is a time when we we can discover who we really are, and what we can really do.

Untie the Knot in Cannot is a book intended as an introduction to understanding how were socialized and indoctrinated into society. There are many authors that I would encourage my readers to pursue:

- Miguel Ruiz—author of *The Four Agreements* and subsequent books Many of his teachings are included in my book
- Wayne Dyer—Though he is now deceased, I still religiously watch his videos on YouTube, and listen to his books on Hayhouse
- Joe Dispenza and Bruce Lipton
- Deepak Chopra
- Sir Ken Robinson—offers many insights into our current educational system

With the help of these esteemed authors, "Susan" was born: Susan who was programmed, conditioned, socialized and domesticated to believe that she was a failure. In the end, she emerged victorious, no longer the victim of her conditioning. I embrace Susan, congratulate her as Susan's story is actually my own story. It is the story of many women who still remain victims of their socialization. Their golden Buddha is still encased in the clay, ready to be chipped away.

But my story does not end with this book; I am still transforming, still transcending my past and it is a glorious journey.

Remember that "We are kept from the experience of Spirit because our inner world is cluttered with past traumas. As we begin to clear away this clutter, the energy of divine light and love begins to flow through our beings." ~ Father Thomas Keating

THE GOLDEN BUDDHA IS WITHIN EVERYONE OF US

How do we remove the clay and stone that is covering it to reclaim the essence of who we are?

In 1957, in a monastery in Thailand, a large crack was discovered in a large clay Buddha. Once the monks chiseled away at the clay, a beautiful gold Buddha was revealed.

Apparently, a few hundred years ago, an attack by the Burmese army was imminent. The monks decided to protect the golden Buddha by covering it with clay. When the army saw the huge clump, they decided it was useless and left it unscathed. After a few centuries, the story about the statue was forgotten until 1957.

Carolyn Tate, who tells the story of the Golden Buddha, offers insights into this story. She explains that the Golden

Buddha is inside each of us. But, over the course of our lives, we pile layer upon layer of clay over our Golden Buddha. She maintains that the heaviest layer is the result of our own doing and by unconscious conditioning.

Through, enculturation, domestication, and socialization, the clay turns to stone and is difficult to eradicate. Though we are born with the Golden Buddha inside of us, we forget that we are blessed with it until there is a breakthrough in our lives when we can begin chiseling away at the hardened clay.

Many of us spend our lives searching for a purpose in life, all the while reliving the negative tapes of our childhood. We forget that our purpose is within us. We just need the right tools to chip away at our conditioning to find it.

In *The Daily Stoic* (a book of daily readings) Seneca, the great philosopher wrote of A cure for the Self. The question for the day was posed:

"Don't you deserve to flourish? Wouldn't you like to be great of soul, filled with confidence, and invincible to external events? Wouldn't you like to be like the proverbial onion, packed with layers of greatness?"

Susan

Susan could be you, your neighbor, or your friend. But she is, indeed, me. My struggles, and feelings of inadequacy stem from my socialization. It took many years to chip away at the clay that hid my Golden Buddha. Remarks from parents, teachers, and partners were deeply embedded as they were internally repeated over and over in my mind.

The tools used to eradicate faulty beliefs about myself included meditation, visualization, journalizing, and reliving painful memories from an adult perspective. It entailed a long process of removing negative energy from my system to eventually embrace my Golden Buddha.

"Whether you think you can or you think you can't you're right."

~ HENRY FORD

Our Belief System is the Accumulation of

SOCIALIZATION
INDOCTRINATION
DOMESTICATION

Being immersed in various classrooms as a substitute teacher, I have been privy to some of the most hateful words from students on a daily basis. Not only are words directed to their peers, but the most dangerous targets are themselves. I worked with students with behavior problems at the high school level. No matter how hard I tried to encourage them with short videos, posters, positive affirmations and group time, the prevailing belief was that of failure. "I'm a loser." "I'll never amount to anything." "The world would be a better place without me." "I can't do this work." If a student believes he cannot do something, he will not try; others will not expect him to perform. To overcome their feelings of inadequacy, they would immerse themselves in alcohol/drugs, video games or other self-destructive behaviors.

The internalization of believing they were failures took years. The repetition of "You're a failure" from the parents and guardians became a reality: The students gave up and didn't try; they indeed failed. And so the self-fulfilling prophecy took place: You tell me I am a failure>> I will fail>> you point out that I am a failure.

Our socialization stresses the concept of "doing." We gain value as a human being when we accomplish things; we get approval from others if we can do better than our peers. We get rewarded for our deeds. "We are what we do." (Wayne Dyer). We are defined by our accomplishments. So, if we don't "do," then we don't get rewarded, we don't get approval, and we lose our value as a human being. Children crave approval from their parents and their teachers; if they don't get it, they can give up trying: their "doing" is rejected. Their self image now is one of failure.

Dyer also stated that most people have been raised to believe what they cannot do. They end up being deprived of what they deserve in life because their attention is focused on what they can't have and what seems impossible to them.

Our individual belief systems are so strong that they surpass the reality of our physical or mental handicaps. We limit ourselves by our beliefs that we are incapable of achieving. We are constantly being told by those we admire, that we are not "good enough"; therefore, their evaluation of us must be accurate. Somehow these erroneous beliefs need to be eradicated. But before we can change a belief or a behavior, we need to change the reinforcements, the pay-offs for not striving.

"Children are not things
to be molded,
but people to be unfolded."

~ JESS LAIR

Susan's Socialization

It is said that for every negative remark, it can take up to twenty positive remarks to offset that one. So many of us will internalize all the criticisms and toxic comments while discounting a compliment. So how can we offset years of conditioning and socialization? I was deeply perplexed when my fiancé, after reading the first few pages of this manuscript, stated that most people have feelings of insecurity stemming from their childhood socialization. It made me more determined to do more research on this topic. A colleague commented that Susan's story stems from the input from her parents and she reiterated that she remembered how fortunate she was that her parents encouraged her to succeed and gave her emotional support. However, as an adult, she was still filled with insecurities and regrets over decisions she made raining her own children.

So, I began talking to women who raised by well-meaning parents or guardians and still suffered from insecurity and a sense of worthlessness at a later age. However, other women came from totally dysfunctional households where alcohol/drug abuse was common and yet became successful, resilient adults. I began to focus on the perceptions of the women—how they interpreted their socialization; how they perceived the influences in their lives.

Susan entered into my life last year, experiencing anxiety attacks and much self-doubt about her endeavors. Susan was sixty-seven and wanted to find fulfillment in her life.

She had no idea as to where to find it and she was petrified at the thought of spending her golden years in a rocking chair, while life passed her by. I was very much intrigued by her life story, and was surprised that such an accomplished woman would feel so insecure.

Susan was the product of the socialization process of "I am never good enough." Her father was a strict authoritarian, demanding that she get good grades in school (He was an English Professor) and wanted her to succeed in education). Her mother was a gorgeous woman who instilled in Susan to always look her best. From the outset, Susan couldn't measure up to her parents' expectations. She was an imaginative child, always playing make-believe. She couldn't seem to keep her room tidy: it was always in disarray. Her efforts to please her parents seemed futile and resulted in years of bed-wetting. The word "can't" was her closest friend. She "knew" from the time she was little that she would never amount to anything. She had no talents: She couldn't sing or draw; She was too clumsy to dance or be in sports. She was afraid of water and so she couldn't swim. She recalled that in Junior High the music teacher asked her to lip sync as she was so off-key. It was ironic that throughout her life she had such a love for music and knew nearly all the words to the popular songs that she couldn't sing them (unless she was in the shower!). Her Physical Education teachers expected her to excel in sports as she was so tall, but she was just too uncoordinated.

She did find some humor in her clumsiness : "Sir Ken Robinson made the comment in one of his Ted Talks years later that intellects have bodies just to transport their brains. He even provided the mental image of a group of teachers (after a few drinks) all gyrating on the dance floor. I tried to imagine other adults such as myself, stilted beings with no rhythm moving across the floor!"

"I'm full of self-doubt. I doubt everything I do. Everything I do is a failure."
~JOHN BANVILLE

Her belief system rendered her a victim at an early age. She was a chronic bed-wetter up to the age of seven. She always knew she was different, that she didn't fit in. It was ironic that while this belief system dictated that she was indeed a failure, she would daydream of becoming somebody great: She fantasized about one day gazing in the mirror at a beautiful graceful swan instead of the ugly duckling that she was. But, the reality was she had no talents or abilities to make that transformation.

I asked her about her earliest childhood memories. Susan started crying, remembering how she would have frequent temper tantrums and how she would make up excuses as to why she couldn't do what was expected of her. One night, as she was in bed, she overheard her parents discussing how she was so much like her aunt. This terrified her, as her aunt was mentally unstable.

She took refuge in reading. Her first year in school introduced her to a magical world of letters transforming into words and sentences, and finally the wonder of stories. Reading made it possible for her fantasy world to expand. She would conjure up stories to go along with the characters in the books like *Dick and Jane*." She dreamed of becoming a writer. Her teacher was her mentor, her guide: She 'got" Susan's passion and kept challenging her. Susan absolutely adored her.

One memory really stood out from this period in her life. She had a particularly successful day at school and was looking forward to sharing the experience with her parents. Her older brother picked up after school on his bicycle. Susan remembered sitting on the handle bars, feeling the wind whipping through her hair. She was exhilarated. This was one of the few happy memories of her childhood. (I made Susan repeatedly conjure up this memory when she was feeling really despondent).

She remembered looking forward to being in second grade. She wanted to see what challenges her new teacher would present to her. Now her sense of worth was tied to understanding numbers and calculating sums and differences. She couldn't fathom the abstract concepts of math: where were the familiar tangible number cubes and blocks that her first-grade teacher utilized? She began to dread going school: Education now became her enemy. She would sink into her seat when the teacher returned papers to the students; She knew hers would be filled with those red marks, pointing out all her mistakes. There was no kudos for her reading. Now she was judged also on her penmanship, which was sloppy.

Because she failed at math, she believed she was a failure. She hated school. She hated her teacher. To make matters worse, she couldn't communicate her feelings at home. She was told she would just have to study harder. She was still wetting the bed and was afraid to go to sleep at night.

It didn't get any better. Her fourth grade teacher demanded that the class copy everything she wrote and drew on the board. It had to be perfect. She would painstakingly draw a picture of a tree and insist that each student's "tree" had to match hers.

But Susan never saw trees that matched her teacher's drawing. She would close her eyes and "see" her trees in her yard; she delighted in drawing trees as she saw "trees." This only incurred her teacher's disapproval. Susan couldn't replicate what the teacher had drawn. So, in front of the entire class, her drawing was torn up. The message was clear: "Don't think for yourself. You have to obey others who know better than you." Her penmanship was usually messy and almost every endeavor at copying the neat letters on the board was met with more red marks across her papers.

"Flowers are red, and green leaves are green. There's no need to see flowers any other way than the way they always have been seen."

~HARRY CHAPIN

In the short video *Flowers are Red* a student goes to school, eager to learn, to paint the world in all the vibrant colors he experienced. But his teacher continuously admonished him with the above quote until the student conformed to the teacher's views and lost his desire to learn. Even when the student moved to a new school where his teacher embraced diversity and welcomed "colorful" depictions, he was so indoctrinated by his previous teacher, he could not regain his zest for vibrancy. He kept repeating his teacher's words that he must only paint "flowers red and leaves green." Surely Susan's teacher was an excellent example of how to stifle a child's individuality.

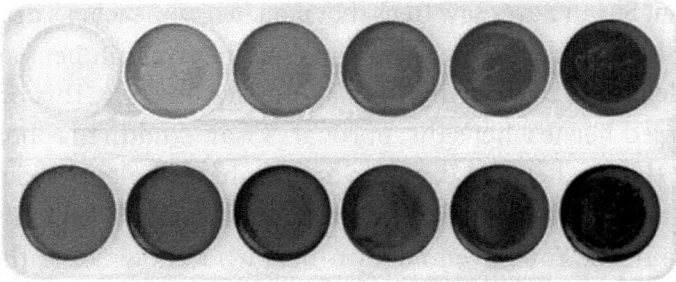

Susan broke down as she recollected one art lesson. She had been given a brand new set of Reeves's paints and sponges. She loved the separate colors and how by dipping the tip of the sponge in in water and then into the colors, she could see the magic on the paper. She was so careful to not mix the colors in her new set. But then, to her horror, the teacher stood at her desk and dipped the sponge into her paints, splashing the colors into one another. Susan had to follow her example, dipping the sponge into the colors and then onto the paper to create a sponge painting of a tree. After school, she threw the paint set into the trash can. It lost its allure: "It looked hideous to me, with all the dried up colors mixed together. "

So now she had another reason to believe she was a failure. She couldn't draw and her printing was still messy. To reinforce these beliefs, the teacher would hold up examples of the excellent work of her peers followed by her papers as the examples of shoddy and inferior work

She remembered sitting in classroom throughout the years, terrified that she would lose herself. She tried to focus on what the teachers were saying but she couldn't concentrate. She would have time lapses wherein she would "lose" up to 10 minutes of time. She would be listening to the teacher and then it would be ten minutes later. She completely blacked out.

"Teachers would yell at me, telling me to pay attention. As always, I was so mortified when my classmates would chuckle at the many reprimands. I felt like my mind was a kaleidoscope; the harder I tried to focus, the more my mind would wander. Always there were so many thoughts racing and interrupting whatever tasks were at hand."

More proof that she was a failure: She was labeled as the child who couldn't pay attention. The immature child. And the list goes on.

"I developed various coping mechanisms. I would lose myself in books, becoming the main characters in my imagination. I would write for hours, conjuring up all kinds of plots. My fantasy world became my "safe" place to go when the pain of the real world became too unbearable. I filled my mind with all kinds of "going to do's". I was going to write a book; I was going to keep my room tidy. They never transpired into anything that got done. My father labeled me the "gonna" girl—the one who was always gonna do something.

If I mentioned to him something I wanted to do he would tell me to come back when I finished it."

Her writing came to an abrupt halt when her father came across her writings and having been an English teacher, decided to critique them. "He went over each story with me, making those dreaded red marks to denote mistakes, and telling me how childish my writing was. I remember throwing all those papers in the trash, the realization that I was a fool to think I could write anything worthwhile burning through me. To this day, I still have that memory which has become the belief that I am not a writer. Even when, in later years, this belief was challenged, I never gained any confidence in my ability to write."

Reaching adolescence and going through puberty was a time of confusion and pain. Because she was an emotional child, she was beset with conflicting emotions on a daily basis. At times she believed that there was something wrong with her. No adult stepped in and validated her feelings, that she was just a "normal teenager".

Somehow Susan made it to high school where she faced new obstacles: French and poetry. "I realize now that I could not possible learn another language when I could not hear the flow of words. I never heard the difference between stressed and unstressed syllables. I had trouble, and still do, understanding languages and accents. My attempts at speaking French in class were dismal to say the least. I stumbled over every word. I couldn't analyze the rhythm of poetry and I often wondered if this affected my inability to dance: I couldn't seem to maneuver my body to the beat of the songs.

When it came time for Susan to graduate, she was at a loss as to what I was going to do, "I didn't have any clerical skills and I had no interest in any of the traditional jobs. So my father insisted that I get my teaching degree. However, when it came time for me to do student teaching, I dropped out of the program. How could I be in charge of an entire classroom if I couldn't be in charge of myself?"

When the Student is Ready, The Teacher Appears

So where was I supposed to go now? What was I going to do? My indoctrination into being a failure was now set in stone. I could not eradicate those voices pointing out all my shortcomings. Alcohol helped for awhile, allowing me to wear my mask of self-confidence. But, it soon began interfering with my ability to work. I would sabotage almost every job that I had which in turn made me drink more. I became involved in abusive relationships and started a downward spiral that lasted almost twenty years."

Those years were the darkest years of Susan's life. "It took so much energy to pretend that I was okay to the rest of the world, especially my parents. I knew my father was disappointed in me; he expected so much more from his daughter. I still took refuge in reading, now perusing all the self-help books that were on the market. I did not want to do the work to "find myself" so I naively hoped that in one of those books, there would be a magic formula to cure me. I did go to a psychologist but I had to quit when I had to be candid about my feelings: I couldn't let anyone in on my shame of being a loser."

Finally, at the age of forty, she hit rock bottom. She had nothing to show for her life. Her husband of three months had disappeared in the middle of the night while they were staying with his friends. They were in the midst of moving and all their belongings were in the U-Haul. He took everything she owned, including her identification. "My friend who took me in said that the only direction I could go now was up. But I was still abusing alcohol to mask the pain, and I couldn't see how I could move up from nothing."

"But life throws us unexpected curves. I met a man at a local bar who had two special needs teenage sons. I began dating him and then moving in with him. One day he brought home a brochure from the local college. He knew that I always wanted to write and the college was offering a Writing Lab class over the summer. I signed up for it even though I was terrified at the thought of anyone reading what I had to say. When I walked into the class, I realized I was the oldest student there, and the only available desks were in the middle of the room. When the professor began her lecture, I realized I was in the wrong class! This one was a basic writing class for college—it was not for creative writing. But I couldn't walk out —I knew everyone would be staring at me. But I decided to stay in the class because I had nothing to do that summer, and I loved learning."

"There are moments that mark your life, moments when you realize nothing will ever be the same and time is divided into two parts, before this and after this."

"An ordinary lecture, nothing spectacular, just a lesson on grammar, specifically where to insert commas. Ms. W. wrote on the board "Tomorrow, and tomorrow, and tomorrow." Without thinking, I blurted out "Creeps in the petty pace from day to day to the last syllable of recorded time." (Shakespeare's Macbeth) When I realizedvisible. The entire class was silent; Ms. Walker just stood there and stared at me."

"But then it happened! In one moment, my entire life was transformed. Ms. W. began clapping her hands and stated that she was amazed at one of her students in a beginning class would be familiar with Macbeth. She kept me after class, and asked me all kinds of questions. Throughout that summer, she became my first grade teacher, my mentor, my guide. She encouraged me to excel in her class. I was back in my first grade class! I was encouraged to succeed; my professor actually believed I would succeed!"

At the conclusion of the summer session, Ms. W. referred Susan to a counselor who worked with "re-entry students", students who returned to college after a long absence. He said he saw a spark in her eyes and wanted to see her soar. He encouraged her to enroll in classes that fall. "My transforma-tion into a successful college student was amazing. Though I had to study harder than my peers (taking copious notes, typing lectures that I had recorded, and making flash cards), my college experience was exhilarating. I fell in love with psychology, sociology, mythology, and literature. I lived and breathed learning." But, even though Susan was getting good grades, there were always these voices saying she wasn't good enough, that eventually she would fail. She enrolled in the next level basic writing class and on the first day she had to provide a writing sample in order to stay in the class. "I knew the reputation of Mr. C, and of how strict he was. My legs were shaking when he called me up to desk. He held up my paper and said "You don't belong in class." I couldn't look at him and started to walk toward the door when he said "You are much too advanced for this class."

What Susan accomplished in the next ten years in academics is amazing! She started a club on campus called the RASCALS (Returning Adult Students Club and Learning Society) Many of the members had felt like they were losers growing up; some had dropped out of high school; some got married early. The members held tutoring sessions for each, babysat each other's kids, and provided transportation to and from college for those who didn't have any. For three years they were each other's support system. She moved on to get her Bachelor's Degree and then her Master's Degree (she graduated valedictorian).

While in school, she looked after her two teenage stepsons, (both with fetal alcohol syndrome), and worked part-time at college. She then went on to get her teaching Degree and took classes in special education so she could glean more insights about her stepsons' condition.

She worked as a Resource Specialist and taught Language Arts at a Middle school. After she retired, she was an Independent Study Coordinator at An Adult Education facility. She also counseled women at local Indian Reservations.

And here she was at my desk, discussing her feelings of insecurity and anxiety over what she wanted to do in her remaining years. "For once, I want to do something that I am passionate about, something that will truly give my life meaning." She broke down and began sobbing. "All I know is education but just because I am good at it doesn't mean that I derive great pleasure from it. The saddest part is I don't have any idea about what would give me that passion I crave."

I asked her about her childhood dream to become a writer. "Until I was told it was a childish dream, that I had no talent.

I don't know if I will ever get rid of those negative tapes."

Susan's parents were not abusive, emotionally or physically. They provided a good home for her and by all measures, provided a standard middle class environment. Her father's parents either were incapable of, or chose not to, display affection. So now, being a parent, he was emotionally distant to his children. Susan's mother had been brought up in poverty and wanted to give Susan everything. She stressed the importance of always looking her best. She was overprotective of Susan, and tried to treated her like a little girl. Both parents had the best intentions for her, but the message they sent to Susan was "You are not good enough."

I can only rely on Susan's recollections which I know can be misconstrued. Statements made by her parents could be remembered out of context. But, the messages she got from her parents, along with her school experiences, did have a dramatic effect on her.

What I gleaned from Susan's story is that the love she received was perceived as conditional love. "I will love you if you get good grades/look your best." When we receive conditional love, we can never measure up to our parent's expectations. We crave their love and end up doing what they want, losing our authentic selves in the process.

It was Susan's socialization that led her to wonder what her life was all about. While she did have much success later in life, it was meaningless to her because of the motivation that led her to succeed. Her achievements stemmed from having to prove herself, having to please her father. Her obsession with her wardrobe and outward appearances mirrored her mother's. The motivation to succeed was not intrinsic.

Susan's story does have some closure, however. Her father

had since passed but her mother was still alive. Before her father passed, he asked her if she still hated him (at one time, she did not speak to him for a number of years). She told him that her education had provided her with choices: She could go through life being a victim and being on the proverbial Freudian couch for years, bemoaning her childhood or she could examine her father's domestication—having parents who never showed him how to be affectionate and raised him with conditional love. She chose the latter, and was able to understand her father) I convinced Susan to discuss her memories with her mother. The ensuing conversations were definitely an eye-opener for Susan: Her perceptions of her upbringing were not in alignment of how her mother remembered her upbringing. Her mother tried to instill in Susan a sense of self-pride, and confidence. She stated that she truly loved Susan and did the best she could raising her. After some time, she talked about her own childhood, her own insecurities. Susan felt she was in her mother's shadow, being the daughter of such a beautiful woman: it was Susan who felt she could not measure up!

Susan's story is by no means unique. After I listening to her, I interviewed approximately fifty adults, ranging in age from eighteen to seventy. Only a handful seemed to reach adulthood and beyond, unscathed by their socialization. Some, admitting that they had less than supportive parents or guardians, stated they weren't affected by it. After all, nobody's childhood is perfect. But, the majority of those I interviewed still carry with them the negative tapes from their upbringing, either at home or at school. They still carry with them, the belief that they can't (can't pursue a childhood dream, can't go back to school...). The grown-up adults are still perceiving their world from the view of a child. They are stuck with their "cant's" and are unable to move on.

As I pored over the notes from my sessions with Susan, I felt that familiar anger along with sadness over how we can be indoctrinated into believing that we can't measure up to society's standards. I felt angry because I knew it doesn't take much to instill self-doubt in a child: A raised eyebrow, reminders to cease "wrong" behaviors", statements such as "You'll never amount to anything," take their toll within a short period of time. I felt sadness because, while it was so obvious that Susan, while achieving so much success in later life, still felt unworthy in so many areas. She still did not believe in herself. I am concerned about my students becoming just like Susan.

IF STUDENTS LEAVE SCHOOL LESS CURIOUS THAN WHEN THEY STARTED, WE HAVE FAILED THEM.

#INNOVATORSMINDSET

HOW SCHOOLS
DOMESTICATE US

Our country embraces the concept of individualism; however, our school system is rooted in conformity. We don't embrace our naturally different and diverse population. Sir Ken Robinson has written books on Education along with many lectures on *Ted Talks*. He sees the many flaws in our current Education practices and offers solutions. In his book *The Element* he provides many examples of how Education has failed students. He gives the example of how two of the Beatles band were told to give up music! Students need to be engaged and stimulated in order to learn. Instead, in most cases their curiosity is stifled. I wonder if Susan was stimulated and engaged in her learning process, she could have thrived.

I see so many students who do not fit the mold: some of them entered the school system eager to learn, curious about everything, asking all kinds of questions. But then their questions stopped and they learned to conform. Many of them can't sit still in the classroom; their hands are fidgeting and their minds are wandering. What if they were engaged in a meaningful, hands-on activity?

There are so many innovative teachers in the Education system. Their rooms are filled with positive affirmations; the students are praised for their work; yet, it is not enough. They follow the curriculum that is mandated and the time lines for teaching it. However, there is great diversity in the learning levels of the students. Some are grasping the information, while others fall behind. Then, there are the "problem" children, those who are disruptive in class, interrupting the learning of others. These are the ones I am concerned about.

These are the children who, by now, realize they will not succeed. They have been told this many times by their parents or guardians. They act out in the classroom and on the playground, doing what children do to get attention. They participate in the school programs to deescalate problem behaviors in the school, but they are not internalizing. It is not enough to combat the messages received at home, and now by other students.

"Because we cannot, our masks show we can."

As I said earlier, there are so many of us who have stories similar to Susan's. We are socialized to fit into society and to strive to meet others' expectations, only to fail. As we trudge through life, we learn to wear masks to hide our insecurities. The masks are our persona of success, shouting to who will listen, about our perceived achievements and hiding behind our labels of Doctor, Professor, CEO, and so on, plastering our walls with degrees and certificates. We can't let anyone see behind this façade. Our entire identity is forever linked to what society expects of us. Removing our masks renders us vulnerable: Surely others will reject us of they see who we really are. But this is the paradox: our masks attack similar masks. People faking it to impress others who are faking it. There is no opportunity for genuine love and affection—just the stroking of each other's egos. And here's the irony; when others compliment us, we can't accept the praise because deep down, we know we don't deserve it!

Our masks hide our striving to meet expectations of others, especially those of our parents. Many of us are on the impossible journey of trying to please a parent who has passed away many years earlier. We are stuck at the age we were at the time of our parent's death. We go through life still hearing the words of disapproval in our heads. In *Into the Woods* the scene of Father and Son reveals this predicament : They (our parents) disappoint; they disappear. They die but they don't." And so, "the farther you run, the more you feel undefined for what you've left behind." The scene depicted "life father, like son"—the son exhibiting the same behaviors of the father who had died years earlier. Trying to live up to their expectations is a trap; preventing us from living the way we want to. Our quest to please others is fruitless and exhausting. Miguel Ruiz sums this up "If each of us could love ourselves as we wish to be loved, then we wouldn't let our hunger for love make decisions for us."

So powerful is the need to please those who domesticated us, they become our subconscious. They dictate how we will respond in certain situations, what decisions we will make. In the movie *The Story of Us*, the main characters Kate and Ben are trying to find meaning in their deteriorating marriage. In one scene, both sets of parents are manifested, becoming the puppeteers of their children. Ben and Kate responded to each other's comments regurgitating their parent's words. By the end of the movie, they were each able to view their situation through their own eyes and reconcile.

Wayne Dyer analyzed the popular rhyme "Row, row, row your boat." Whose boat do we row? Our own, not our parents', not our spouses' and certainly not society's." How do we row our boat? Gently. Life is not a struggle. Where do we row our boat? Down the stream. Not fighting the upstream of life. So we do this merrily. Why? Because life is but a dream!" I have this rhyme on a sticky note one my mirror to remind me not to take life so seriously. And, after all, it is my life not to be wasted on trying to please others. One of Miguel Ruiz's four agreements is "Don't take it personally." This was a difficult one for me to internalize: All my life I took everything personally! But now I realize that I am just a bit player in everyone's play of life. In my play, I am the artist, the director, and the producer. When I finally recognized that I had spent so many years wearing my mask and trying to live another's script was useless because not one perceived me the way I wanted to be perceived. All the drama I had created in my play actually went unnoticed by others. They were, and still are, directing their own plays. And, most important, everyone is responding to their perception of who I am, their image of me, which, of course, is not me.

In his book, *Pairing—Guide to Intimacy* **** the author provides numerous examples of how our attempts to please others while donning our masks is fruitless. In each case, the dialogue of two people is followed by what the person is really thinking. One couple had made an agreement to engage in sex after they had spent a day at the beach. During the day, the woman was sunburnt and did not want to have sex: she asked her companion if he still wanted to go ahead with their plans and he said "Of course." But inwardly he also did not want to be intimate that evening. He did not want to disappoint her. Needless to say, their sexual liaison was unpleasant for both of them. (They both told each other how much they enjoyed it, however!). I can remember countless times of agreeing with others when I wanted to impress them. Much of our dialogue does not reflect about what we are really thinking.

In one of my Marriage and Family Class, I asked my students to write a eulogy of their loved one. They had to list favorite pastimes, passions, disappointments, and achievements. This was very difficult for most of my students. Either their partners had shared the things on the list beforehand and the students weren't paying attention or they just had no idea who their partner really was. One of my students, in her mid-twenties was in a six year relationship. It was almost impossible for her to make a statement or offer an opinion without prefacing it with "Ben...thinks/believes..." I had her write in her daily journal without referring to her partner. After two days, she came to my class crying: she realized that her entire life (choice of friends/clothing..) was Ben's creation. She had no idea where his thoughts ended and hers began.

Once my student started the work on herself, she was slowly transforming into a self-assured young woman, who was beginning to trust her own instincts. Her "eulogy" of Ben was almost one hundred percent accurate. He refused to do one on her. (I was told that months later, they broke up.)

Another assignment I gave my class was that for 2 weeks, the students and their partners were not allowed to watch television or engage on their phones for 2 hours each night. They were to instead, truly engage in meaningful conversation with one another. Sadly, very few of my students could complete the assignment. So many of them really had no sense of who they were and had the erroneous belief that their partner could magically make their whole.

When I was divorcing my husband, he asked me to explain exactly why I was leaving him. First I asked him who I was: what was I passionate about? What were my biggest disappointments? What were my fears? He could not answer me. Then I asked him to tell me when was the last time we had a meaningful conversation. Again, he was silent. (I almost asked him to close his eyes and tell me what color my eyes were! - my mother's best friend of thirty years did not know the color of mother's eyes!) It took me many months to realize that he was not all to blame for not knowing the answers: even in a marriage I was unable to be truly intimate with him. I never let him in. I never shared the "uglies" inside of me.

"Life is an Onion and One Cries While Peeling It."
~ PROVERB

It took years of counseling and inner work to peel away the layers of the "onion" of my insecurities. They were embedded in hundreds of self-degrading thoughts and beliefs. But slowly, I was I able to remove my familiar mask, even though it was absolutely terrifying. Taking off the mask is like being stripped naked, all of me exposed to the entire world. I had to get rid of my identification with my titles, my extensive wardrobe, and all my belongings which I had such an attachment to. In truth, I was almost stripped naked: after surviving the Paradise Fire on November 8, 2018, I was left with just the clothes on my back. I did not have any identity. I had to forge ahead not knowing how I could recover.

I had to rely on my own inner strength and my tools from counseling. I relied on all the books I had saved on my smartphone—authors such as Deepak Chopra, Wayne Dyer, the Buddha—which inspired me to truly "let go." In my book *Phoenix Rising From the Ashes* I remark that I left who I was in the ashes of the fire, giving rise to a "new me." A me that is constantly evolving, changing with each experience. It is my mission to help others evolve also, without the impetus of a catastrophe.

One of my favorite books is by Jess Lair "I Ain't Much Baby, but I'm all I got." It took a catastrophe for him to alter his lifestyle. He was typical successful business person on the fast track of life until he had a major heart attack. When he recovered, he began the process of letting go: resigning from his position, and moving his wife and family to the outskirts of town. He became a professor, encouraging his students to seek authenticity.

I began my quest for overcoming insecurities by interviewing people as I discussed earlier. I kept wondering how many of them had a song, a story, a picture in their heart that wouldn't be shared with the world because of insecurity. Most of them led fast-paced lives, working, entertaining, taking care of family. They had little time to reflect on their lives, to examine their life choices. They admitted to having "childish" dreams early on in life, but matured and strove to be successful, which was having a car, house, and family. A couple of my interviewees were able to follow their passion, but admitted to being ostracized by their friends and family. Success to them was getting paid for something they truly loved, and having time for meaningful relationships.

It takes courage to peel the onion that is us. We know we

have to face that dark side that is buried in ourselves. We may have to recollect painful memories that we have repressed. But once we realize that we no longer have to berate ourselves for our thoughts and actions; that trying to be perfect is erroneous, only then can we embrace ourselves and truly communicate with others who are facing their own demons. Only when we realize that we are okay just the way we are, we can drop our masks and be authentic.

Our culture embraces individuality. We are socialized to be strong and forge ahead no matter what. Yet this belief is a paradox: those who embrace their individual thoughts and beliefs are sometimes ostracized; so many of us just conform with the rest of society—again, which means hiding who we really are.

Once we begin the process of peeling the onion, we lose the status of being a victim of our past. Deepak Chopra state that we become educated about our limitations so our view of the future becomes distorted. We become prisoners - I read an analogy to show how we imprison ourselves: The prisoner is in a room filled with darkness, with only one window that allows the sunlight to enter the room. The prisoner spends his time reaching for the sunlight, trying to see what is outside, while ignoring the door that is encased in the darkness.

I Cannot Live Up to Society's Expectations

Culture is the umbrella of society. It dictates what we wear, how we interact, and what we value. In the western culture, we are socialized to value and embrace the youth. We spend billions on creams and operations to offset the natural process of aging. Make-up and concealers are the most common masks women don each day to hide the telltale signs of aging.

i have to be per

Our work ethic dictates that we sacrifice our family life for the good of the company. We work long hours, endure long commutes, and pretend that we are successful. The harder we work, the more we buy, and the more we live beyond our means. Appearances are crucial: having the perfect house, car, and career. The cocktails and pills taken to sustain this lifestyle keep us rooted in this façade. We have lost touch with what many of us call "Our inner child." That part of us that once strived to do something in life, to create something; that part that got squelched by adults telling us let go of those dreams and become useful. After all, it is the goal of socialization to train children to be "functioning members of society." But the more we ignore our true nature, the more our masks begin to crumble, as we develop physical, emotional, and mental problems. Our identities become what we are and what we do not who we are. "I am a doctor." At one time I worked as a career counselor for CEO's who lost their jobs due to downsizing. These men were stripped naked and vulnerable: They now had no identity. How could they be a husband and a father if they could not provide for their families? Their masks were ripped from them and they were terrified.

> "In civilized communities men's idiosyncrasies are mitigated by the necessity of conforming to certain rules of behavior. Culture is a mask that hides their faces."
> ~ W. SOMERSET MAUGHAM

The tragedy of striving to meet the needs of society, our culture, is that we are forfeiting the basic premise of what it means to be an American "individuality". We conform to the "certain rules of behavior" because what would happened if we didn't? Would we be shunned? Would we lose everything that we have been striving for? Sadly, many of us stay on the treadmill of life, conforming to society and wearing our proverbial masks.

However, the masks of society are definitely crumbling. The pharmaceutical business is thriving, consumers relying on pills for all kinds of emotional and physical ailments. Our entertainment idols are beginning to look like cookie cutters—flawless skin, perfect figures, hair extensions all radiating youth. It is a race against time and they are losing.

Untie the Not
and Let the Light In

So, to return to initial dilemma: What can we do, if anything, to combat the indoctrination of "not being good enough?' My research led me to the Japanese doctrine of *Wabi-Sabi*. Each piece of pottery that is created has a "flaw" in it. The Japanese believe that pottery with its flaws is even more beautiful after going through the process of being broken and repaired. The flaws represent events that happened in the life an object. This philosophy transcends to real life. We all experience shame, rejection, failure, etc. So we don our masks, lest the people around us see our flaws. They would see that yes, we are not perfect, we are not good enough. We become, like a flawed object, hidden in a cupboard behind all the "perfect" china.

WABI-SABI

(n.) the discovery of beauty in imperfection; the acceptance of the cycle of life and death.

But we really have a choice as to how we perceive our flaws. We can forever, hide ourselves behind our masks, pretending that we are "perfect"; we can wallow in self-pity and blame others for our perceived failures or we can see them as "golden seams."

> "Ring the bells that still can ring
> Forget your perfect offering
> There is a crack in everything
> That's how the light gets in."
> ~ LEONARD COHEN

None of us finishes our journey unscathed. All of what we have endured, defines us, makes us who we are. It is a tragedy, that by wearing masks, we deny others the opportunity of others to see our inner beauty.

I realize I "cannot" untie the not in cannot embedded in our cultural beliefs. I can only go out into the world, naked and vulnerable "Hi! My name is T.K. and I'm all I've got."

A few weeks ago I attended a women's conference where on woman after another "bared their souls" to a receptive audience, each one reliving their unique socialization experiences. Their demeanor, physical appearance, and clothing masked the years of pain they endured. But each one of them, with the help of a mentor, religion, and their own inner strength overcame the feeling of not being good enough and embraced their flaws (from the experiences) as their own golden seams. I know there are thousands of conferences and meetings taking place around the country, each with tales of brave and vulnerable people.

Right now we are in the midst of the pandemic. Those of us who need help in chipping away at the clay that hides their Golden Buddhas are isolated and shut off from those who could help them. More than ever, we need access to the resources that can help people access their Golden Buddha. I have created a website where I have shared my own journey since the pandemic started. I also have included a resource page where readers can share resources and inspirational books. It is my hope this can help those who are unable to reach out to others.

I have recently joined a Positivity Group: There eight of us who meet once a week to share positive thoughts and insights. We encourage each other and offer uplifting thoughts. The ages of the women range from forty-five to eighty-three; the differences in age completely disappear during our sharing! We are all on the same path of enlightenment. To most of us, this group is the only time we interact with others because of the social distancing.

I am now being trained as a mentor in Medford, where I can hopefully connect with our troubled youth. The Covid Virus, along with the fires, has affected our children in so many ways.

One of my favorite authors is Wayne Dyer, who has since passed away; but he has left such inspirational messages to us all. (I share his books and quotes with anyone who will listen) He uses the term "source" in lieu of the Golden Buddha, telling us to reconnect with our source and obtain bliss in our lives. He stated that when we are discouraged, or sad, we are disconnected from our source. It is when we are aware of this that we must reconnect with our source; actually we are never disconnected to it. We just need to return to it.

My therapist, who was instrumental in alleviating my anxiety disorder through muscle testing, encouraged me to read *Letting Go* by David R. Hawkins, M.D.,Ph.D., an extensive study of becoming free of negativity. He claims that when the "I cant's" are removed, whole new areas of life are open to us, that success stems from doing what we love. The ultimate goal of letting go is total freedom. The book provides us with the verbiage to us when we are talking to ourselves and others; techniques are provided, techniques that we can easily implement into our daily routines.

Now that I have chipped away at my socialization and indoctrination into society, I am becoming much more empowered. I question opinions and remarks made about me (how I dress, what I believe in…); As Miguel Ruiz states "Don't take it personally." Letting go has made my life so much simpler.

It is my goal now, to help others remove the negative blockage in their lives and transcend the "I cant's in their lives." We can travel the same path together.

> I have shared my tale with you.
> Will you share with me?"

Website: TKBanner.com

About the Author

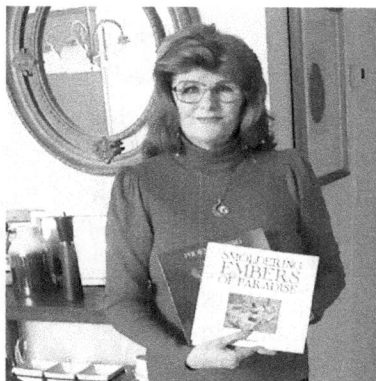

T.K. BANNER is originally from British Columbia, Canada. She has been an educator her entire life—teaching first grade through twelfth. She also taught Sociology at Mount San Jacinto College in California for over twenty years. After she retired, she became the director of an Independent Study Program for Adult Ed for eight years.

She and her fiancé bought their dream home in Paradise, California in July 2018, only to have it go up in flames four months later. She relocated to Medford, Oregon, where she is substituting at the local schools. She is the author of two books *Phoenix Rising From the Ashes* (her ordeal the day of the fire in Paradise) and *Smoldering Embers* the sequel to Phoenix Rising From the Ashes.

Her current book *Untie the "Not" in Cannot* stems from years of trying to help children and adults alike find some meaning in their lives. She examines our culture and our socialization which demands perfection from us.

OTHER BOOKS BY T.K. BANNER:

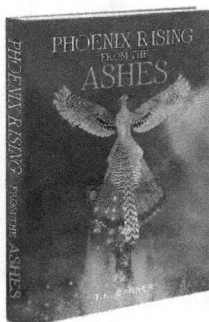

Terry Banner was a lucky survivor of the Paradise Fire in 2018. She, with other teachers, protected their students as they fled for their lives in a schoolbus, driving through a wall of flames in the fast-moving fire.

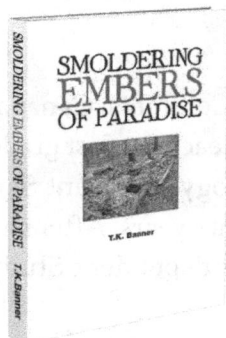

In her unforgettable memoir: *Phoenix Rising from the Ashes,* and sequel, *Smoldering Embers of Paradise* are a first-hand account of the destruction of Paradise, and inspiration for those who are confronted with tragedy in their own lives.

www.ingramcontent.com/pod-product-compliance
Lightning Source LLC
Chambersburg PA
CBHW060622030426
42337CB00018B/3155

BACKSLIDING
IN HEART

5 STEPS TO A BACKSLIDING HEART
AND BACK AGAIN

BY

BRIAN MARK WELLER